But What About Hunter Biden!?

As Russian tanks rolled through Berlin...there were still those who cried out to their Fuhrer, *save us, save us from what you've done!*

As Rome burned...there were still those who called out to their Caesar, Nero*, save us, save the city from what you've done!*

And today, as Washington crumbles...there are still those who cry out to their orange god...*only you can save us from the disaster you created!*

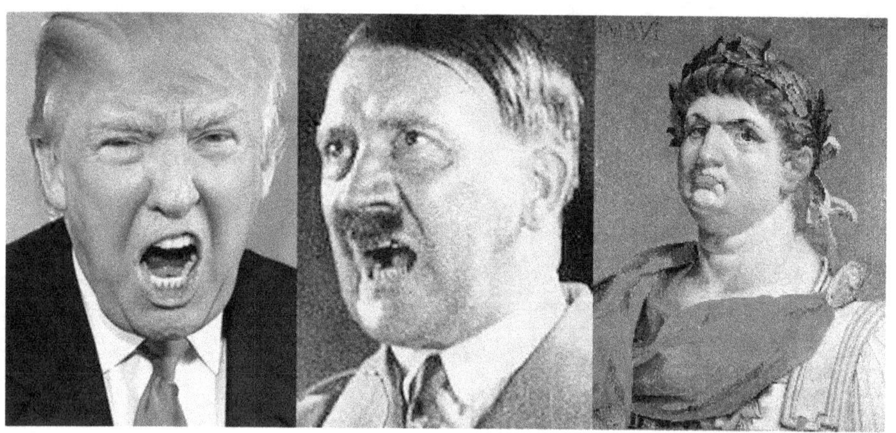

We live in strange times...

Historic times...if not terrible.

!!! But what about Hunter Biden !!!

Why?

This is Part IV of a series that I really had no intention of writing but somehow feel that I must.

I typically write fantasy books with various levels of sexual involvement…but even some of my best works can't match the insanity of Trump and the world he and his misguided, undereducated misfits have plunged us into.

As I've said before in my other books of this nature, when George Bush Jr left office…after getting us into two wars, destroying the economy and essentially damaging the GOP so badly that it has yet to recover and now possibly never will following the idiocy of Trump…you couldn't find a Bush voter anywhere. No matter how many rocks you turned over, no matter how many beds you looked beneath…they were nowhere to be found. The man had somehow won two terms without a single person in the fucking country voting for him…it was a miracle.

Talk about voter fraud…Jesus.

But that wasn't really the case. In truth, once he had gone, his supporters simply looked the other way, erasing all involvement and blame they had for electing the man...and we simply let them do it, perhaps believing that they had learned their lesson.

Then they tried to vote in Sarah Palin as the VP and we all nearly shit our pants.

Luckily, that nightmare never happened...and again, we let these people simply vanish.

They certainly learned their lesson after that...right?

FUCK NO!!!!!!

Hold our fucking coffee was their response.

As if to show their stupidity knew absolutely no end and had no bottom...we were handed Trump.

And because he won...at least in terms of the electoral college, having lost the popular vote, those with their IQ just above their shoe sizes...fell in love with a maniac.

And most of them still are, even after 2 impeachments, 4 indictments, (so Far,) being found guilty of sexual assault, and 4 post Presidency years of pure fucking insanity that never seems to end.

Hell, we even just learned recently that he openly discussed nuclear secrets with an Australian businessman...just because he wanted to...

But his cult still loves him.

However...

With all that said...

They won't always love him...not all of them.

Before it's all over, most will see him for the criminal conman that he truly is...then they too will slither away, leaving behind only vague memories of hate and racism...and a closet filled with his Nazi-style souvenirs.

And we will simply let them...right?

Well, not me.

This book, along with the three before it of the same nature, are meant only as a keepsake. A time capsule if you will. I wish to preserve just a fraction of the hate and blunderous stupidity that envelopes these Hate Monsters...so we never forget who and what they were.

That is my goal.

And so, to meet that goal, I present to you...But What About Hunter Biden!?

Enjoy.

Now, before we get into this, I'll explain how this works.

Essentially, all this book contains is news articles taken from various sources about various things, usually political but not always. What I do, after providing a brief summary of the article, is take the comments of those on the right...and put it in here...simple. To protect the identity of those providing the hate and insanity within their remarks, I do not provide any last names. So, for example, if someone gives the name, Alex Smith, I will simply remove the Smith...leaving it Alex. Also, due to certain issues involving my computer, I also delete most, if not all, emojis...my computer won't accept them for some reason. Aside from that...these remarks are pure and simple, the words of Hate filled, horribly misguided individuals...for your enjoyment...and fear.

Oh, and from time to time, for the really crazy ones, I will leave a remark of my own.

Now you know...

So...let us begin.

Xi, Putin detail 'deepening' relations between Beijing and Moscow during conference in China

Russia-China trade climbed to $200 billion in the last year, Putin said.

ByKarson Yiu

October 18, 2023

ABC News, Online

HONG KONG -- While one war continues to rage in Ukraine and another is threatening to boil over in the Middle East, Chinese President Xi Jinping held court in Beijing for visiting dignitaries, presenting his vision of "an open, inclusive and interconnected world" through his signature global infrastructure project, the Belt and Road Initiative, while taking veiled swipes at the United States and its

Western allies.

Dan M.

 Biden is too busy wanting ban guns that hold 100 rounds in the chamber. No such gun exist.

Chuck M.

"An open, inclusive and interconnected world", like an open border. He sounds just the Democrats in this country.

Tom R.

Biden did this.

Rob G.

Brandon's weakness on the worlds stage is a large part of what's going on!

Alonzo H.

Only on BIDEN'S watch...

Mohamed P.

Sure they are great world leaders at least they don't have dementia like the US dead mummy Biden .. who died long time ago may his soul rest peace

Mike S.

THE WORLD WAS SAFER AND BETTER UNDER TRUMP...FACT!

....And that's how we do this....

This next article is about a new Russian offensive in Ukraine. Now, as I write this, Republicans have become so incredibly brainwashed by Trump when it comes to Russia that they have even begun to wish complete defeat upon Ukraine in their war to remain a free country? Why, well, that's something for them to explain...so let's see what they have to say...shall we?

ABC News

ByPatrick Reevell

October 23, 2023,

.

Russia has thrown thousands of troops and hundreds of tanks and armored vehicles into launching a new offensive against Ukraine.

Ukrainian officials on Sunday claimed that Russia had lost more than 6,000 soldiers in a week, as well as over 400 armored vehicles and tanks. Britain's defense intelligence claimed Russian casualties have spiked by 90% since it began the new offensive.

Ok...so, let's see the Right-winger educated Trump-fed response to this.

Garrett D.

We are being fed lies lies lies and more lies. It is all the American Media does

Chris C.

Ukraine is getting demolished right now and it's beautiful.

I looked at this man's profile and he claims to be 100% American…apple pie and women in the kitchen GI joe kind of guy…but here he is rooting for our enemy because his orange messiah (Trump) has him completely lost.

Antonio K

Remember everything the media says is usually the other way around.

Again, hoping we are the ones losing…if only by proxy.

Karl S.

Glad we live in a country where citizens n the streets arm themselves. Military won't have any weapons or ammunition left over to protect us with by the time we get invaded because we gave it all to other countries.

Gilberto B.

Emphasis is on "Ukrainian officials claimed"

Wayne C.

That's about how many illegals cross our border everyday.

6000 every day…I guess there's nobody left in Mexico.

Don P.

Western media good in telling lies to their gullible readers and listeners

Fake profile…god only knows who this guy is…sure sounds Trumpish though.

Chris B.

Prove it???

Greg P.

Hey! Has anyone contacted Putin about the ecological effects and global warming yet?

Maybe he doesnt know.

William P.

In Hollywood I guess Ukrainian official cannot continue with this media propaganda to show strength...... Russia has already taken what she came for

James G.

Some more fake news.

Ray M.

Are you guys not tired of all this lies you are telling to the public you have all been found out ! That western propaganda doesn't sell anymore

This special person lives here in America but he's using the Phrase, Western Propaganda, probably because the Russian bots are...so it sounds good to him I guess.

Maisam S.

LONG LIVE RUSSIA

WE STAND WITH YOU

It is self defense

Russia Invaded Ukraine...

Jowee Z.

 ABC media propaganda producers pushing the corrupt political marketing narrative again to give America □□a false perception that ukraine □□is effective in winning the USA □□proxy war against Russia □□to justify printing more fake war dollars to fill the pockets of the corrupt oligarchs.

 America is $33 trillion dollars in debt . Our monthly payments can barely cover the debt interest rate. We are broke! Stop printing fake war dollars and stop the media war propaganda marketing

Always follow the money

Is this guy Russian...is he American? Private profile....

--}

 Ok, now let's dive right into the heart of crazy...

 Trump.

Trump fraud trial live updates: Cohen details how he says he inflated Trump's statements.

By Peter Charalambous and Aaron Katersky

ABC News.

Former President Donald Trump is on trial in New York in a $250 million lawsuit that could alter the personal fortune and real estate empire that helped propel Trump to the White House.

Trump, his sons Eric and Don Jr., and Trump Organization executives are accused by New York Attorney General Letitia James of engaging in a decade-long scheme in which they used "numerous acts of fraud and misrepresentation" to inflate Trump's net worth in order get more favorable loan terms. The trial comes after the judge in the case ruled in a partial summary judgment that Trump had submitted "fraudulent valuations" for his assets, leaving the trial to determine additional actions and what penalty, if any, the defendants should receive.

*This article is about Trump's former attorney and fixer, Micheal Cohen, who went to prison for Trump on various tax violations...the same ones Trump is now on trial for.

 Let's see what the Trump cult has to say about this...

Ursula J.

Trump brought PEACE !!!

Biden and his administration brought War, Incompetence, Division and Corruption!

Biden ended a war...isn't the one on trial for corruption, and hasn't gone around declaring that half the country's population is the enemy of the people...like Trump has and continues to do.

Lisa M.

So a convicted liar is testifying against an innocent guy - OK!! Liberalism Is A serious Threat to America!!!!

David Hale

The civil trial? The one the AG couldn't find enough evidence on to bring criminal charges, so she punted and went with a civil trial? The civil trial where no bank or other financial institution is claiming they were defrauded, because they were all paid in full? That's the trial this known liar and perjurer is testifying in? #Trump2024

There isn't a single bank in America that will do business with Trump.

Brendan G.

These are power hungry people

Lock your children up

Fire cops teachers and nurses if they won't be force vaccinated

Investigate impeach arrest you before you become president then work against America for 4 years

COMMUNISM in AMERICA

Craig M.

Don't care, still voting Trump.

Chase K.

Only democrats can deny election results.

? Does he even read the articles...or does he just chime in with random right-wing rhetoric to feel better about himself?

Jonas T.

So, we are supposed to believe Cohen who served time for federal campaign finance violations and tax evasion? LOL We all seen Trump's Tax return. But the left will side with him because Trump will lower your bills once he regains leadership.

Terry A.

Cohen is a liar.

Terry R.

Here piggy piggy .. bacon bacon bacon ..

Piggish Democrats have to manipulate a take down. By way of the judicial system, to remove President Trump from the election. A Vladimir Putin, Russia Russian tactics. 📱 And they have to do this by September 2024 or Trump wins the election. Tick-tock tick-tock, time is running out .. little piggy's

Justin F.

I hope Cohen lies under oath and gets caught and screw up the no case as it is. Cohen is a known pathological liar.

Don D.

The prosecutor's entire case is based on Cohen, a convicted perjurer and fraudster. Boy aint that a hoot.

Angie W.

All of you Trump haters, he has done more for the country then Biden ever did, Biden is a traitor and corrupt, the truth will prevail. Biden used airforce 2 to transport his son to do his businesses with other countries, our tax dollars hard at work.

*Here we go...some pure What About Hunter Biden shit at work here. Guess she missed the 4 years of Trump's daughter lover and her fake Jew husband jetting around the world to enrich themselves on the American tax dollar.

Jon W.

Yea Cohen is credible he hasn't lied on the stand before.

Jowee Z.

No one cares

 ABC democrat media propagandists still throwing americans 🩸🩸 tampons because corrupt Biden is bleeding at the polls

Biden Democrats funding millions to ABC on media propaganda marketing campaign against trump, republicans and just wasting tax payer money because trump or no trump corrupt Obiden family will never ever be re-elected for 2024 presidency

Jay A.

Biden should b in jail not trump

Gram B.

support trump

Lj R.

A convicted felon and a former employee these political witch hunts are ridiculous.

Carl O.

Trump 2024

John M.

Wait, a convicted liar takes the stand define irony.

----- It Gets scary, doesn't it, how filled with blind hate and pure stupidity these people are.

--}

How about something to do with the circus that is the Republican MAGA led House of representatives and their 4th attempt to find just the right criminal for the job…

The House is set to make speaker votes at noon, according to the official notice to members.

By Alexandra Hutzler, John Parkinson, and Lauren Peller.

ABC News.

The House is voting for its newest speaker candidate, Rep. Mike Johnson. He is the fourth nominee for the top job after the historic ouster of Kevin McCarthy earlier this month.

Johnson, a hard-liner who won his party's nomination Tuesday night, will work to get the 215 votes he needs to clinch the speakership.

The chaotic battle for the gavel has dragged on after House Majority Leader Steve Scalise was nominated, but backed out when it became clear he didn't have the votes. Last week, the conference dropped

Rep. Jim Jordan as their nominee after his speakership bid failed for a third time on the House floor. House Majority Whip Tom Emmer had the nomination for less than a day before he dropped his bid Tuesday evening.

 Let's just see what the crazies have to say....

 Snehaah K.

Doesn't Stops Trump Win □p

I speak for all we're voting Trump

 Snehaah K.

.

Biden worst president in history ☐ ☐

Biden will be in jail come 25 Jan2024

Two in a row by this potential Russian bot troll.

Joyce R. L.

Democrats cant wait to get someone in there so they can spend more money. Take your time. They just want to pass the 106 billion to fund wars. Warmongers just make fun and talk about trump can't see what their president is actually doing.

John P.

2024 the year the Patriots destroy the liberals.

 Carol H.

I sure hope he gets elected house speaker. Time to move on. Our country is going into the pits with Bidens dementia.

---}

Not too many comments on that one…yet, so let's move on to another…older story…that one was too fresh, the crazies hadn't come out yet. Let's just do a Biden story…even something innocent and simple should bring out the lunatics…

How about this…

Pres. Biden welcome Australian prime minister at White House

HAPPENING NOW: Pres. Biden welcomes Australian PM Anthony Albanese at the White House.

 *This isn't even an article, it's just live footage of the President getting ready to meet another country's President. (Prime Minister.)

Let's see the hate this brings out....

John E.

How much money is Australia going to ask for and for what every time somebody meets with the president he gives money

Judite J.

His playing with his tie

*She had 3 laugh emojis after this because I guess Biden adjusting his tie somehow means something...idk.

Janet M. H.

He's the biggest joke of a president. Let's go Brandon

Liz S

Biden rewriting history AGAIN. ☐☐☐☐Dr Biden ?

No idea…?

Kat R. P.

I wonder if he's pooped his diaper yet?

Judite J.

A lider his not its a secret who's running our country

Uh…what?

Lian G.

As our counties child are eating out of dumpsters if eating at all. Allies are not feeding our hungry!!

How dramatic…guess she believes her orange god would somehow end world hunger if he was back. You know, because there were no starving people while Trump was in office…at least in her head.

Kelly L.

Two peas in a pod An embarrassment to our country.

Her profile picture is that of a girl essentially groping herself...but she wants to tell us all about whose an embarrassment...hmm, curious what her father thinks.

Brian D.

Joey has us supporting 2 wars. 0 wars with Trump. There have been 13 attacks on American camps in the Middle East this past week. Why hasn't joey said anything about it?

Probably because he doesn't get his news from conspiracy sites like this guy does. And what 2 wars is he talking about? I'll give him the whole Ukraine thing...but what's the second?

Steven S.

he is too old - i have many friends that voted for him in 2020 know they say they made a mistake and are going to vote for DONALD TRUMP in 2024

Penny L.

Biden is the Worst president ever

Judite J

His he sleeping standing up

*Guess this simple meeting really upset her…this is her second semi-understandable comment.

Mary X.

They can't management the country or Speak ….Simple retirement

*This girl, if she is a girl, has the image of a AI Japanese semi-nude girl as her profile image…such class.

Kristiina K

Jill Biden has serious mental problems. The world needs to see Jill Biden in a mental hospital.

Georgia D.

Biden Mc TRAITOR

Amanda K.

My god Biden, pay attention to what is going on.

Erica Miller

He is ridiculous

Scott F

Joe is sleeping

Bob R.

What about the border

There's always at least one of these...why doesn't he go protect it from all those dangerous non-Republican Mexicans?

Lian G

Fix OUR country first

Diane A Z.

The man of war

Susan B.

Oh he's awake.

Dave C.

I see Biden is on a stage, hope there's a ramp and not stairs

Bryan O

Gov. NEWSOME just kicked you to the curb

? No idea…sometimes they're so dumb and misinformed that there really is no answer. I have no idea what this was about…though I doubt he does either.

Vijaykumar H.

Biden must discuss with the Australian counterparts how to protect the southern border and continue to build the Wall.

This guy lives in India…he forgot to change his profile information…oops, no check for him from the Trump pac that hired him.

Nick Zimmer

So glad Mike Johnson is going to be speaker no more money sent to Ukraine or Israel time to work on the American people and end demorats reign

Michael C.

The president of the liar & thief club welcomes the prime minister to the greatest circus in the world.

Lea B.

Wow what a show for a visitor! How much did this cost Americans! Never seen this ever!

Gary A. J.

JOE BIDEN IS A GENOCIDAL MURDERER!

*Jesus...

---------------------- *I'll leave it there. Just the site of Biden welcoming someone at the White House brings out this much hate...amazing.*

 Now let's get into something the MAGA Republican clowns care about more than anything....Private citizen Hunter Biden.

 This should be crazy.

Bombshell Update on Hunter Biden Special Counsel Testifying

American Insider.

Story by Carver Malone.

*This story comes out on the weekend when the far-right always seems to take over the media...when the real reporters go home leaving the B-team in charge of the playground...that's when this kind of story typically breaks.

The House Judiciary Committee, responsible for the investigation of Hunter Biden's illegal business dealings and his father's political corruption, has revealed that it will now be interviewing the Department of Justice's Stuart Goldberg and U.S. Attorney for the Central District of California Martin Estrada regarding the alleged politicization of the DOJ.

*This is the House of Representative's pointless investigation into Hunter Biden led by the criminal Jim Jordan.

"Burisma, I think, captures it all," Jordan pressed.

Hunter Biden gets put on the board and gets paid a lot of money. Fact No. 2: He wasn't qualified to be on the board. Fact No. 3: The Burisma executives asked him, 'Can you help us with the pressure we are facing?' Fact No. 4: Joe Biden gets [Ukrainian prosecutor Viktor Shokin] fired—leveraging American tax dollars to accomplish that."

*Hunter was already charged with tax fraud and made a plea deal with the DOJ...so, in truth, none of this means a damn thing and never will...but that's the MAGA GOP in a nutshell.

Let's see what some of the crazies have to say about this waste of time and taxpayer money….

V P.

Put this crackhead in Prison.

This person has the image of a black slave as his/her profile picture…why, who knows?

D K

So many crimes on the laptop to put Hunter Biden away for life where is the squeeze on Hunter Biden to turn on Joe Biden like they are doing to Trump?

Alan D.

Ok we all know he's guilty stop all this and convict him.

Douglas L.

Criminals will face justice.

Stephen D.

Joe and Hunter are NOT above the law. Lock them up

Larry S.

The walls just keep closing in.

VALERIE M.

OHHH, I think he should just go to the beach with Daddy, while the worlds in major turmoil

*? What?

rob r

Private interview??? You mean the interview that we are paying for and deserve to hear every word of?

*They can't show the interview to the public because everything they have tried to do and show about Hunter Biden has blown up in their faces, including fake whistleblowers, foreign spies, and flat-out bullshit liars.

pine a

Put this low life and Daddy in jail already. We all know if their last names were Trump they would have been in jail years ago.

ron t

put them in jail

Ed B.

LOve it, Bombshell and don't forget "the walls are closing in". LOL (Sarcasm) Nothing will happen to Prez boy. The FBI will stop it.

He's kinda right...nothing will happen.

Claudia B.

Convict him and put him behind bars.

Robert W

Bidenomics in action:

US gives money to Ukraine

Ukraine gives Hunter a no show job

Ukraine pays Hunter $83,000/mo

Hunter "rents" Joe's beach house for $50k/mo

Hunter keeps $33k.mo

Joe makes more than his presidential salary.

Bidenomics = money laundering

P M

They will keep stalling till Brandons out of office

Ted W.

It cannot be more obvious. If a criminal went in front of a jury for murder and even though they did not find the body, if the evidence was overwhelming, as we have with the Bidens, that killer would be convicted, as has been many of the cases over the years. Sadly, only a tunnel vision biased person would not want to see the truth even if it was right in front of them.

It's as if he's explaining himself but is simply too dumb to see it...remarkable. Jim Jordan having a feeling and talking to a handful of fake whistleblowers and foreign spies is not exactly what one would call evidence...which is why this case as a whole has not gone anywhere beyond a simple tax crime and gun charge in nearly 7 years.

 CURT R. S

Can we say "treason"???

Old man Coleman

Bet this article will bring out the demorats saying show me the evidence. It's there but dem voters who voted for this convict for president watch to much CNN and that waste MSNBC. The dirtbag is guilty.

D K.

Treason pure and simple.

D H

Much like Joe and Hunter, Biden voters are minor-attracted.

Carl A.

Joe will be found unfit to stand trial.

Silverback S

any body else. An officer + on drug test is a dishonorable discharge. Biden reach far and deep

tony h

My bet is that Obama knew what Joe did and helped make it go away as a story.

*This guy still hating on Obama...wow

---------- *The Hunter Biden rage runs deep and touches a nerve with these people...but they don't care at all about Donnie and his crime family...all of whom, as I write this, are set to go to trial over tax fraud in NY and will almost certainly lose their business licenses there. But Hunter smoked some crack...so lock him away.*

I'm just gonna put this here...you know, because that's the face of a sober man right there...lol

Moving on....

This next article is about the GOP led House of Representatives and their decision to place a MAGA extremist in as speaker...

Opinion by Rex Huppke, USA TODAY

If you care about democracy, or about abortion rights or about the lives, freedoms and well-being of LGBTQ friends and loved ones, this past week was important.

If you believe the 2020 presidential election was free and fair, as has been proven time and time and time again, this past week was important.

This is an extremist political party with no intention of untethering itself from its often-courtroom-bound leading presidential primary candidate, Trump. This is a political party willing to lie and dissemble and win at any cost to push an agenda wholly out of line with the views of most American voters, as evidenced by the GOP's struggles in the last three national elections and in smaller special elections across the country.

Johnson makes clear his dislike of the separation of church and state

As soon as he won the gavel, Johnson stood in front of the speaker's chair and said: "I believe that scripture, the Bible is very clear that God is the one that raises up those in authority, he raised up each of you, all of us. And I believe that God has ordained and allowed us to be brought here for this specific moment and this time."

Days later, he told Fox News' Sean Hannity, "Go go pick up a Bible off your shelf and read it. That's my worldview."

Mike Johnson is as big a MAGA election denier as there is, and he never backed down

Beyond Johnson's desire to hoist his faith upon the masses, he was and, as best I can tell, still is an election denier. He fought tooth and nail to build a ludicrous legal case seeking to overturn the 2020 presidential election results in four key states, and he voted against certifying Biden's win.

He has never apologized for that undemocratic sham. After being named House Speaker, Johnson was again asked if he still believes the election was stolen. He wouldn't directly comment, saying only: "My position on that is very well known."

Comparing Roe v. Wade to Hitler's 'judicial philosophy'

This all sounds bad, but we've barely dipped a toe into Johnson's extremism.

He once suggested Roe v. Wade was negatively impacting the economy: "If we had all those able-bodied workers in the economy, we wouldn't be going upside down and toppling over like this."

Let's see what the crazies have to say.

Aaron B.

Democrats were the ones that made Johnson Speaker. If Democrats had not voted to remove McCarthy then Johnson would not be Speaker.

Democrats only have themselves to blame.

McCarthy started a completely pointless impeachment inquiry into Biden despite no evidence of a crime even being committed.

Gram C.

Ever notice anyone that disagrees with the Democrats is labeled an 'Extremist'....

Shalon P.

Awesome! Cant wait for the Republicans to take over Congress and the White House and start throwing Democrats in prison. Its going to be a wonderful time. The only extremism in this country is coming from the Left. That is a fact. Most of the mass shootings in this country in the last few years have all been leftist democrats.

The crazy runs deep with this one.

joseph g

It's not like 208 democrats partnered with Gaetz and 7 other
Republicans, that they supposedly despise, to make this all possible.
Sounds like buyer's remorse to me.

Fred B

Maga Extremism? Lower taxes, smaller government, energy
independence, defending our borders, fiscal responsibility........This is
what the average American wants.

J Craig

There they go again. It is the Democrat party that has given in to the
extreme leftist agenda.

Jo B

Thank you, Biden, for screwing all those seniors that were dumb
enough to cosign student loans for young Biden voters that defaulted.
And now the seniors are having those payments deducted from their
social security checks.

Jay S

Cultist democrats, driven by love of fascism start up with the same refrain they always use. The GOP will destroy the nation. Unless 10% is allowed to keep the southern border open. Print more money than ever in an attempt to start ww3. Rule by executive order in place of following the Constitution. These are but a few samples of the reasons why Biden in at 31% approval. Trump leading in all polls but one. People see democrats are not just globalist in nature but fascist in temperament as well. Old rex went from chicago trib to USA today. Talk about sinking fast.

Larry M

more untruth from media. Democrat Marxist at work ling with every breath, sending a once great Country in to extreme destruction.

C W

When you're continually affronted by Leftist extremisms in every way imaginable, what other result could you possibly expect? Moderates, like me, have no choice but to lean even more to the Right to counterbalance the extreme policies that come out more and more each day. Transgenders stripping in front of the WH, reparations (seriously?), open borders, BLM marching on behalf of Hamas, ultra liberal colleges, DEI and ESG in investing, Bidenomics misinformation, tossing around trillions in spending, free education through forgiveness without Congressional approval, killing domestic oil production, fed gov trying to run capitalism, and the list goes on....

Noel S

The WOKE calling another MAGA is the Democrats way of demonizing its opponents rather than presenting a valid argument.

First time we've seen that word, "WOKE," in here. That's the word right-wingers use to describe anything and everyone they disagree with. They've back down from it a little as of late after Florida Governor and Serial Dog Shit Sniffer Ron DeSantis began to look like a raging madman for using it on virtually everything…but this guy is still pounding away with it.

robert k.

Thanks USA today for accusing anyone that wants secure borders, limited or no wars, safer streets, fiscal responsibility and inflation under control and policies that favor Americans first, as extremists. Shows where you stand.

None of these people cared about the border till Trump told them it was the most important thing in the world…now it's a counter phrase to everything. Republicans put a MAGA madman in as Speaker… "oh, yeah, well, a trillion Mexicans just crossed the border yesterday, so there."

Thomas R.

does anyone reading this ridiculous garbage realize that the left KEEPS SAYING making America great is a BAD THING and extremist??? The davos people and the chinese are all over this and most of you are too blind to see it...wake up before its too late

Edward A

Look at what is important to democrats: Abortion and LGBTQ rights. compared to what is important to republicans: God and family. I'm for the wholesome side.

Kenneth C

thank you Jesus for this stop gap against evil...!!!

James S

One of the most insane opinions I've ever read. Do you think he hates Trump? Sounds like a leftist propaganda speach.

Kenneth C

extreme??? open borders is extreme!!!

Like I said...they use this like ketchup on bad food.

dennis c

USA Today is such a left wing rag.

Chris C

Just another example of Fake Leftist articles by USA today

John B.

THIS headline is 180 degrees opposite of the truth. This last week Middle America won in the U. S. House of Representatives.

You think this guy has any clue what he's even talking about? I doubt it.

---}

Alright...let's see what the crazies have to say about Israel. As I write this, Israel, in retaliation for a Hamas rocket attack that killed over 1,000 Jews, is steamrolling the

Gaza Strip claiming there is a war being fought...

Now, I feel it is important here to remind you, the reader(s), that a significant portion of Trump's base...are Neo-Nazis and/or white supremacists...and, beyond that, Trump never seems to find the

courage to ever truly separate himself from these people in any significant way, including referring to Charlotsville Neo-

Nazis as... "Good People."

Let's just see what these people have to say about the current situation...

President Joe Biden pressed his Israeli counterpart to "immediately" scale up the flow of humanitarian aid into Gaza, and a top Israeli official told CNN as many as 100 trucks a day could soon be moving into the

enclave.

By Kevin Liptak and Betsy Klein, CNN

Washington

CNN - President Joe Biden's administration this weekend pressured Israel to allow more aid into Gaza and to restore internet connectivity to the enclave, a concerted effort to ease a growing humanitarian crisis that comes amid fears of a widening regional war.

In Biden's first phone call with Prime Minister Benjamin Netanyahu since an expanded Israeli ground operation in Gaza began, the president "underscored the need to immediately and significantly increase the flow of humanitarian assistance to meet the needs of civilians in Gaza," according to a White House summary of the call.

Valerie W.

I don't know why I feel Biden's words are empty threats.

Davee O D

Biden can barely "press" the button to go up or down on the elevator..

Scott D.

Joe has protected every other border and funded every other country but ours. We will soon have a war in our backyard

*Another border humper...

Mustafa J E

Let us speak clearly. War is an American decision by Biden's godfather, President Obama, and the goal is to end Netanyahu's rebellious future, as Benjamin rebelled against his people, destroyed the judiciary, did not concede in the West Bank, and fought his political partners. He also had a very poor relationship with Obama, and now Obama, with his cooperation with Iran and Russia, has taken revenge on Netanyahu forever. .

Mohamed A.

He is big liyer. Both are meaning of destructions

Netanyahu and Biden must be brought to the International Criminal Court immediately

Martin B C

In the form of missiles two war criminals together both need locking up

Keita B

Hell just waiting for both of these two men.

William W

If today Zionist controlled US government stopped paying billions of US taxpayers money to Zionist government of Israel, they won't be able to fight with bare handed Palestinians

Ebtisam B

Joe Biden's false statements previously caused the killing of a million Iraqis... and now we are repeating the same scene... false statements from Israel and America make Israel commit genocide against the Palestinians...

Paul D.

How about standing by our allies instead of allowing pro terrorist protest happen in our own country...

Trader to the country

You think this guy remembers Trump abandoning the Kurds to be slaughtered...or cares that he tried to blackmail Ukraine which ultimately led to them being invaded by Russia?

Hunter H.

In summary, the people who claimed Trump would destroy the economy, increase racism and start WW3 have crashed the economy, increased racism and started WW3.

Trump did destroy the economy, did increase racism and the Ukraine war can be traced straight back to him. Hell, you could even say that handing Syria over to Russia and Iran led to Hamas receiving missiles and funding for this war.

A O

Why do you call it pressing when he(Biden) is the one remotely controlling the bombardment on Palestinian children's heads?

Michael L

The left is mentally ill. The radical left is FUBARed.

William D

Call it what it is: Massacre and colonization. Israel created Hamas themselves by bombing and shooting civilians, kidnapping and imprisoning Palestinians and stealing their land for decades. The Palestinians has the right to defend themselves from a terrorist apartheid regime.

S and G

.

Lots of typos in this story so I fixed
it...
...............President Joe Biden pressed his Israeli counterpart Iran to
"immediately" scale up the flow of munitions into Gaza, and a top
Hamas official told CNN as many as 100 trucks a day could soon be
moving into the enclave.

Gino H

He is scared. He lost all his voters .. now the world is voting against him
, China snd Russia got there boats near him .. it's a mess. Netanyahu is
putting all his citizens at risk , specially when he said stopping Hamas if
more important then the hostages .. people in Israel and his cabinet
asking for his resignation.. ITS A MESS. Lies , propaganda without
proof.. sleepy Joe need to retire

J s.·

Biden should be concerned about our borders.

But like he says, he just follows the orders.

Those dangerous Mexicans…

Michael S

Biden..shut the hell up....it's easy for you to backseat drive and yell Israel what to do from 3000 miles away I'm the safety of the white house

They need to do what they must do

Hamas triggered this and Hamas claims to be the leaders of the Pakestinians...go urge them to care for " their people" who they threw into harms way

Lawrence D

Why isn't CNN covering the Democrat corruption in the House? Dem minority leader, Jamie Raskin has been ordered to apologize to the House and American people for lying and acting as the Biden family defense attorney instead of doing his official duties ethically and unbiased?

D. K

Biden, the criminal, is like the person who kills the dead person and then walks at his funeral as if he is sad for him like others.

Peter L

Humanitarian aid to put a bandaid on the genocide Biden enabled. He's out of office in 2024!

Steve Matos

If the draft ever comes back there should be about 81 million people ready to defend their King BIDEN.

Weird, the only one who ever speaks of himself as a King...is Trump.

O. O. W.

The world with Joe Biden :wars conflicts instability

Ron A

Joe Biden is an 80 year old career politician gone senile.

M D

Biden is helping Israel to kill kids in Palestina

Pure Crazy.

Janet T

How's this for an idea war-monger Biden - tell Israel military aid will stop immediately. Biden is as phony as a three dollar bill.

John J

"Joe Biden does not project strength. He projects weakness and the rest of the world knows it." - Ben Shapiro

What do you think he thought Trump projected...you know, as the world laughed at us for 4 years.

Scott T.

Joe Lie-Den has sent more support to Iran and Hamas then Israel. That's where democrats priorities are.

April O

Netanyahu is incarnation of NAZI Adolf Hitler!

Redman J.

Biden wants to make sure Hamas has all the supplies they need

Anita B.

Biden can't even talk or walk right! He's not deciding anything!

*Crazy isn't it...these people beg for a civil

war one minute, then blame Biden for wars involving other countries as if they are peace loving little Christians...scary.

*before we move on though...something odd happened as I was doing this part of my book. Occasionally, I will respond to the person leaving the comment...at the source...as I did for one of these people, (I won't say which because of how truly vile this person was.) Anyway, I did just that...responded...and what he responded with was terrifying...but very true.

 In essence, this man was blaming Biden for the war in the Westbank...which isn't really a war, let's be honest here, it's Israel destroying a 3rd world speedbump of a fake country. Anyway, I reminded this man that it was Trump who handed over Syria to Russia and Iran, not Biden, and because of this, Hamas and Hezbollah were handed a direct link to each other, hence Hamas suddenly having much more advanced rockets which they used to attack Israel.

 Well, this man shot right back with what was essentially conspiracy nonsense, blaming Obama and/or Clinton for the entire thing...to which I replied, "What the hell are you talking about? Obama is probably sitting on a beach someplace drinking a pina colada and watching girls in bikinis walk past...and Clinton is like 100 years old and looks like he's an inch from death."

The man replied with conspiracy nonsense.

 So, again, I explained why Trump and his ignorance about what was going on in Syria, where we had all of our enemies and all the terrorist groups in one area murdering each other instead of us, was perhaps the biggest blunder of his entire Presidency...which itself was a clown show.

The man didn't respond at first, and, to be honest, I thought that perhaps he had at least realized what I was talking about...

 But then something very shocking happened.

 The man explained to me that Biden was still to blame...but he wasn't upset about the attack on Israel...oh no, he was upset about what Israel was doing in the Westbank and to the world of Islam.

 Then it struck me...

 This man blamed Biden for defending Israel, (along with Obama and Clinton,) and was pro-Trump because in his eyes, Trump was pro-Hamas and pro-Hezbollah.

By American standards...this man was pro-terrorist...and he was pro-Trump.

 And there were other people, as I continued to read through the comments, that seemed very much of the same state of mind...they hated Israel...but they loved Trump because to them...he hated Israel too.

Example: This is a remark made after an ambulance was bombed.

احمد

Biden's encouragement of Israeli crimes and massacres confirms that Biden is now participating in these crimes against children and women. Biden and the biased American media have fallen morally. We did not see these massacres in Ukraine. It seems that Putin was adhering to the law of war and was confronting the Ukrainian army and did not bomb hospitals.

Israel has now moved to admit its bombing of hospitals, ambulances, and schools sheltering refugees in Al-Ruway. Is old Biden conscious when he accuses the victim?

Remember now...Trump's base is Neo-Nazi.

Is it a Coincidence that these people see Trump as anti-Israel too?

---}

Ok, I have to admit...this is cheating a little. Anything Obama reaches down into the black heart of these hate filled monsters.

But let's do this anyway...

OBAMA!!!!!

ABC News.

ON THIS DAY: Fifteen years ago, Barack Obama was elected the first Black president of the United States, defeating Republican John McCain.

...I could not find any actual article...it was just a historical reminder as far as I could see.

Let's see the rage...

Anita M D

Thought he was the worst president but Biden had that title now!

Joseph K.

One of the greatest days in the history of our country.

I added this one because this was a black man who was serious...he got 81 laugh emojis for this comment...guess from who.

Sandra C.

Miss his decency

Same story as above...black woman being honest...she got 61 laugh emojis.

Don D

Was the beginning of the failing of this country.

Guess he missed the whole 911 thing...and slept through Trump.

Doug S

the start to the end of the united states

Norma M.

The greatest president in history.

45 laugh emojis, 36 hate emojis...

Mike W.

The downfall of the country

Erica D

The day when the extreme division and chaos started.

Kinder M

Selected not elected.

*?

Janette N.

Very sad day for our country.

Kristy P.

And the immorality of society kept plummeting.

Douglas K.

And the country was screwed, ever after......

John D

The beginning of the end for the United States and it's destruction of not only his policies but now those of his VP, Joe Biden!

Marie O

When will he show a real birth certificate?

Ikim N.

And the world especially America has been on a spiral down ever since

Jeremy J

Biggest mistake in all of history! The beginning of the downfall of our country.

Alicia H.

Biracial. And started the division of the country.

Biracial…this is something rather new they have added to their hate arsenal…No idea what it really even means…he was black and white, we all knew that, but I guess they're just now figuring that out…8 years later.

Kenneth F.

The best race baiter ever

Ben M.

America and healthcare has been screwed up ever since

Randy P.

This is the day America became racist again, this is the day that caused everything to go wrong,, !

Wow...just wow.

Joe T.

That thug could a been my son...lol

This is a remark about a black boy who was murdered by a racist for absolutely no reason. Obama once claimed the boy could have been anyone's son, even his.

Shawn M.

What about his German mother?

He was born in Hawaii

Charles H

half white

Joe M

Worst president ever until Brandon came along.

Cary W.

And then we went 8 something trillion more in debt and thousands of Americans lost their lives overseas.

Also, the corruption and politicization of the American government against politcal foes began.

Donna S.

And our problems began. He used our Bible against us while holding his kuran. He used our Christian love to trick us into accepting terrorist and allowing the immigrants to take over

Nothing racist to see here, nah, nothing at all.

--}

Well, before I end this, let's do one more Hunter Biden story…you know, because it never ends with MAGA over this guy.

Hunter Biden is urging the DOJ to investigate a former business associate over claims that he lied to federal investigators about his family's business dealings.

Bobulinski claimed Joe Biden was to benefit from foreign business ventures.

ByLucien Bruggeman

November 3, 2023, 6:09 PM.

President Joe Biden's son Hunter Biden is urging the Justice Department to investigate a former business associate named Tony Bobulinski over claims that he lied to federal investigators during an interview in the weeks leading up to the 2020 presidential election, according to a criminal referral letter obtained by ABC News.

Attorneys for Hunter Biden wrote last month to Matthew Graves, the U.S. Attorney in Washington, D.C., accusing Bobulinski of deliberately mischaracterizing his relationship with the Biden family "for the sake of maligning the character and reputation of [Hunter] Biden and his family, and to boost his own sense of self-worth."

Let's see what the crazies have to say...

Tom T.

Damage control. Guilty

Syarip H

WE ALL LOVE DONALD TRUMP WE ALL LOVE DONALD TRUMP WE ALL LOVE DONALD TRUMP.

No, we don't. (This man is from the middle east.)

Butch V.

Just like daddy always someone else's fault

Gene N.

So can anyone seek probes from the DOJ even if you don't work for the government

Shawn S.

That's it, Blame someone else, that's what demorats do best.

Brad L.

But I thought nothing wrong was done?

Brendan G.

The Commie Biden Family wants the govt investigating their enemies

Biden is funding Ukraine against Russia and Israel against Hamas...who exactly does she think our enemies are, Canada?

Edward S.

The Biden crime family is guilty as sin!

Khadija A.

The US-backed Zionist illegal state of Israel is conducting indiscriminate massacre of innocent women and children in the ongoing Israeli airstrikes in Gaza, Palestine, they are destroying all the infrastructure of a country, schools, colleges, hospitals, mosques, churches, water, electricity are not spared from their airstrikes. , energy, telecommunication system, occupying Israel using 12 thousand tons of explosives in the entire Gaza City is echoing the words of Japan's Hiroshima and Nagasaki in the Second World War, but it is sad but true that the merciless United Nations has failed to take any effective measures to protect the Palestinian Gaza, so this United Nations Who should be called spineless UN?

He didn't name Biden directly, but still, more of these people upset about us/Biden backing Israel.

John T.

THIS DOJ just might. They are clearly weaponized.

Carol K-B

Hunter lies along with the Biden Crime Family

Childress Tracy

Hunter trying to cover up his crimes with the biden crime family.

Kathleen W.

You only want to open this can of worms if you know your daddy is pulling favors.

Jessie R P

They're beating a dead horse just like they did with Hillary. If they were really interested in justice, they'd go after Traitor trump and his spawn.

 A voice of reason…I just felt like showing this.

Olga V.

But,but,but Gunter never received a dime from China truth coming out bud. Sit tight.

Bob I.

Why does Bidet name his kids and dogs "Hunter, Major. and Commander"? He has no idea about the military? The man is a joke!

Almost as bad as an orange clown with bone spurs suggesting that he knew more than the Generals.

Johnny D.

The Biden crime family is being uncovered.

The Biden crime family…that's where I'll leave it because as I write this, the real crime family, the Trumps, are in court giving testimony about how they stole hundreds of millions from banks and creditors in New York.

It never ends with these people.

----------------------------------}

Some crazy before I go...

 Trump and his criminal children are on trial in New York for bank fraud and tax evasion. They have already been found guilty of these crimes so the (trial) is actually to determine how much they owe...and it may be ¾ of a billion dollars by the time it's over.

 So, what's Trump's defense? How are they attempting to defend him...well, you might not believe it.

*Shout out to the MeidasTouch network for the stories and pictures.

Trump's lawyers attempted to say that the judge overseeing the case was a drunk and that his court assistant was bias and essentially running the court. When asked where exactly they got their information, lawyer Christopher Kise replied that he had gathered the information from Breitbart, from a single source with a reputation of false and conspiracy-style stories often aimed at judges and attorneys.

Visit https://meidastouch.com for more!

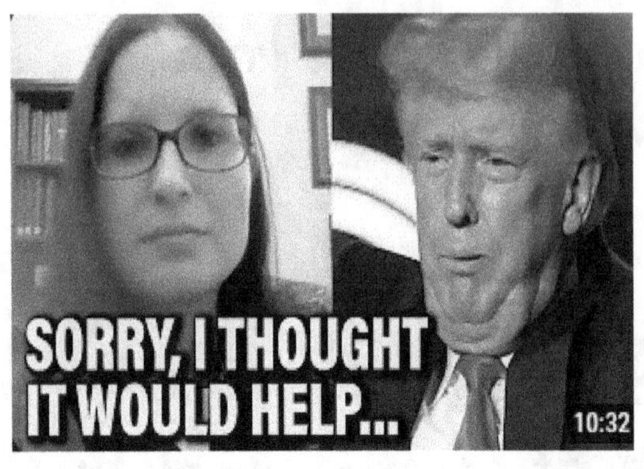

Then, on the flip side of justice, we have Florida judge and Trump appointee, Aileen Cannon.

This lady, all in an effort to defend Trump, has delayed a trial that was and is perhaps the most open and shut case in the history of anything by delaying the trial until after the election. The hope here is that Trump wins and then can pardon himself before the case is ever taken to trial. Remember, Trump was found with hundreds, if not thousands of documents that he had stolen after his presidency ended including top secret documents and documents above top secret. He was heard on recording showing people some of these documents and has been identified in numerous emails where he clearly meant to mislead and lie to the DOJ and the National Archives. In reality...this case, if handled properly by a real judge...should be over already.

Visit https://meidastouch.com for more!

---------------------- The End. ---------------------------------

Other Books By This Author….

FFS.

History is a weapon that villains fear the most.

This is why those that preach hate and conspiracy try so hard to manipulate what our youth learn in school.

Without History, the memories of the madness brought down on mankind by those that wish to enslave and control us…are forgotten.

And the wheel is always turning.

If we fail to record the acts of tyrants and their followers…

Future Generations will be the ones to suffer.

These People.

Never has there been a case in American history so ridiculous as the one we now face, when the dirt-poor worship a criminal conman, some even placing him above Jesus himself. They flock to the polls in numbers never seen before, all desperate to cast their vote for a man who wouldn't piss on their face if they were on fire. I see these people every day, hour after hour, as I work the world of retail. They are easy to spot...they stand out like a black cloud in a clear blue sky. How? It's the hate, it consumes them, creates an aura around them they can't escape...it's the pure hate in their eyes.

All I wish to accomplish with this short book is to create a written time capsule for future generations to see...of a time when hate consumed, and Jesus was kicked to the side by Christians in favor of a man who has spent every day of his life in complete opposition to their sacred 10 commandments.

Hate Monsters.

When George W. Bush left office, he was forgotten. The people who voted for him, his two wars, his terrible economic policies...all vanished. Within weeks of that man leaving office, you couldn't find a man or woman who had voted for him. Somehow, he had won two terms without a single vote...nobody was held accountable, life just went on, the people who had done the damage put their feet up, confident that history would simply forget their stupidity...and they were right. To this day, even in a red state that had voted for him twice, it's a real challenge to find a former Bush supporter.

The same thing can be said of all that have helped terrible men, (and women,) come to power over the ages. After WW2 the military often spoke of the fact that there were no Nazis...that the attitude of the German people was one of shock...that they had nothing to do with the man, he had just risen to power without their knowledge or aid...same with Stalin and Mussolini, they had just appeared...and nobody was to blame.

Enter Donald Trump...and thank the gods...exit Donald Trump. However, unlike times gone past, we now have the ability, with the internet and various outlets of the written word that did not exist in the past, to keep a time log of the insanity, the hate, the people who helped these tyrants, which Trump is, come to power. That's what this book is...a time capsule meant to keep a small amount of the vile hate Trump inspired alive. That way, when he is truly gone, those people, his enablers and sheep, won't be able to shrug their shoulders and simply say...I didn't do it.